CRYPTO CURRENCY TRADING TRACKER

This book belongs to:

_____

_____

_____

CRYPTO CURRENCY TRADING TRACKER

Buy	Sell	Date Time		Date Time		Outcome
Pair		Entry Price		Exit Price		Profit / Loss

Setup

Mental State	Exit Condition

Notes:

Satoshis W/L		% of acct		USD Value	

Buy	Sell	Date Time		Date Time		Outcome
Pair		Entry Price		Exit Price		Profit / Loss

Setup

Mental State	Exit Condition

Notes:

Satoshis W/L		% of acct		USD Value	

Buy	Sell	Date Time		Date Time		Outcome
Pair		Entry Price		Exit Price		Profit / Loss

Setup

Mental State	Exit Condition

Notes:

Satoshis W/L		% of acct		USD Value	

CRYPTO CURRENCY TRADING TRACKER

Buy	Sell	Date Time		Date Time		Outcome
Pair		Entry Price		Exit Price		Profit / Loss

Setup

Mental State	Exit Condition

Notes:

Satoshis W/L		% of acct		USD Value	

Buy	Sell	Date Time		Date Time		Outcome
Pair		Entry Price		Exit Price		Profit / Loss

Setup

Mental State	Exit Condition

Notes:

Satoshis W/L		% of acct		USD Value	

Buy	Sell	Date Time		Date Time		Outcome
Pair		Entry Price		Exit Price		Profit / Loss

Setup

Mental State	Exit Condition

Notes:

Satoshis W/L		% of acct		USD Value	

CRYPTO CURRENCY TRADING TRACKER

Buy	Sell	Date Time		Date Time		Outcome
Pair		Entry Price		Exit Price		Profit / Loss

Setup		

Mental State	Exit Condition

Notes:

Satoshis W/L		% of acct		USD Value	

Buy	Sell	Date Time		Date Time		Outcome
Pair		Entry Price		Exit Price		Profit / Loss

Setup		

Mental State	Exit Condition

Notes:

Satoshis W/L		% of acct		USD Value	

Buy	Sell	Date Time		Date Time		Outcome
Pair		Entry Price		Exit Price		Profit / Loss

Setup		

Mental State	Exit Condition

Notes:

Satoshis W/L		% of acct		USD Value	

CRYPTO CURRENCY TRADING TRACKER

Buy	Sell	Date Time		Date Time		Outcome
Pair		Entry Price		Exit Price		Profit / Loss

Setup

Mental State		Exit Condition	

Notes:

Satoshis W/L		% of acct		USD Value	

Buy	Sell	Date Time		Date Time		Outcome
Pair		Entry Price		Exit Price		Profit / Loss

Setup

Mental State		Exit Condition	

Notes:

Satoshis W/L		% of acct		USD Value	

Buy	Sell	Date Time		Date Time		Outcome
Pair		Entry Price		Exit Price		Profit / Loss

Setup

Mental State		Exit Condition	

Notes:

Satoshis W/L		% of acct		USD Value	

CRYPTO CURRENCY TRADING TRACKER

Buy	Sell	Date Time		Date Time		Outcome
Pair		Entry Price		Exit Price		Profit / Loss

Setup

Mental State	Exit Condition

Notes:

Satoshis W/L		% of acct		USD Value	

Buy	Sell	Date Time		Date Time		Outcome
Pair		Entry Price		Exit Price		Profit / Loss

Setup

Mental State	Exit Condition

Notes:

Satoshis W/L		% of acct		USD Value	

Buy	Sell	Date Time		Date Time		Outcome
Pair		Entry Price		Exit Price		Profit / Loss

Setup

Mental State	Exit Condition

Notes:

Satoshis W/L		% of acct		USD Value	

CRYPTO CURRENCY TRADING TRACKER

Buy	Sell	Date Time		Date Time		Outcome	
Pair		Entry Price		Exit Price		Profit / Loss	

Setup

Mental State	Exit Condition

Notes:

Satoshis W/L		% of acct		USD Value	

Buy	Sell	Date Time		Date Time		Outcome	
Pair		Entry Price		Exit Price		Profit / Loss	

Setup

Mental State	Exit Condition

Notes:

Satoshis W/L		% of acct		USD Value	

Buy	Sell	Date Time		Date Time		Outcome	
Pair		Entry Price		Exit Price		Profit / Loss	

Setup

Mental State	Exit Condition

Notes:

Satoshis W/L		% of acct		USD Value	

CRYPTO CURRENCY TRADING TRACKER

Buy	Sell	Date Time		Date Time		Outcome
Pair		Entry Price		Exit Price		Profit / Loss

Setup

Mental State	Exit Condition

Notes:

Satoshis W/L		% of acct		USD Value	

Buy	Sell	Date Time		Date Time		Outcome
Pair		Entry Price		Exit Price		Profit / Loss

Setup

Mental State	Exit Condition

Notes:

Satoshis W/L		% of acct		USD Value	

Buy	Sell	Date Time		Date Time		Outcome
Pair		Entry Price		Exit Price		Profit / Loss

Setup

Mental State	Exit Condition

Notes:

Satoshis W/L		% of acct		USD Value	

CRYPTO CURRENCY TRADING TRACKER

Buy	Sell	Date Time		Date Time		Outcome
Pair		Entry Price		Exit Price		Profit / Loss

Setup

Mental State	Exit Condition

Notes:

Satoshis W/L		% of acct		USD Value	

Buy	Sell	Date Time		Date Time		Outcome
Pair		Entry Price		Exit Price		Profit / Loss

Setup

Mental State	Exit Condition

Notes:

Satoshis W/L		% of acct		USD Value	

Buy	Sell	Date Time		Date Time		Outcome
Pair		Entry Price		Exit Price		Profit / Loss

Setup

Mental State	Exit Condition

Notes:

Satoshis W/L		% of acct		USD Value	

CRYPTO CURRENCY TRADING TRACKER

Buy	Sell	Date Time		Date Time		Outcome
Pair		Entry Price		Exit Price		Profit / Loss
Setup						
Mental State			Exit Condition			
Notes:						
Satoshis W/L			% of acct		USD Value	

Buy	Sell	Date Time		Date Time		Outcome
Pair		Entry Price		Exit Price		Profit / Loss
Setup						
Mental State			Exit Condition			
Notes:						
Satoshis W/L			% of acct		USD Value	

Buy	Sell	Date Time		Date Time		Outcome
Pair		Entry Price		Exit Price		Profit / Loss
Setup						
Mental State			Exit Condition			
Notes:						
Satoshis W/L			% of acct		USD Value	

CRYPTO CURRENCY TRADING TRACKER

Buy	Sell	Date Time		Date Time		Outcome
Pair		Entry Price		Exit Price		Profit / Loss

Setup		

Mental State		Exit Condition	

Notes:			

Satoshis W/L		% of acct		USD Value	

Buy	Sell	Date Time		Date Time		Outcome
Pair		Entry Price		Exit Price		Profit / Loss

Setup		

Mental State		Exit Condition	

Notes:			

Satoshis W/L		% of acct		USD Value	

Buy	Sell	Date Time		Date Time		Outcome
Pair		Entry Price		Exit Price		Profit / Loss

Setup		

Mental State		Exit Condition	

Notes:			

Satoshis W/L		% of acct		USD Value	

CRYPTO CURRENCY TRADING TRACKER

Buy	Sell	Date Time		Date Time		Outcome
Pair		Entry Price		Exit Price		Profit / Loss

Setup

Mental State	Exit Condition

Notes:

Satoshis W/L		% of acct		USD Value	

Buy	Sell	Date Time		Date Time		Outcome
Pair		Entry Price		Exit Price		Profit / Loss

Setup

Mental State	Exit Condition

Notes:

Satoshis W/L		% of acct		USD Value	

Buy	Sell	Date Time		Date Time		Outcome
Pair		Entry Price		Exit Price		Profit / Loss

Setup

Mental State	Exit Condition

Notes:

Satoshis W/L		% of acct		USD Value	

CRYPTO CURRENCY TRADING TRACKER

Buy	Sell	Date Time		Date Time		Outcome
Pair		Entry Price		Exit Price		Profit / Loss

Setup

Mental State	Exit Condition

Notes:

Satoshis W/L		% of acct		USD Value	

Buy	Sell	Date Time		Date Time		Outcome
Pair		Entry Price		Exit Price		Profit / Loss

Setup

Mental State	Exit Condition

Notes:

Satoshis W/L		% of acct		USD Value	

Buy	Sell	Date Time		Date Time		Outcome
Pair		Entry Price		Exit Price		Profit / Loss

Setup

Mental State	Exit Condition

Notes:

Satoshis W/L		% of acct		USD Value	

CRYPTO CURRENCY TRADING TRACKER

Buy	Sell	Date Time		Date Time		Outcome
Pair		Entry Price		Exit Price		Profit / Loss

Setup						

Mental State			Exit Condition			

Notes:						

Satoshis W/L			% of acct		USD Value	

Buy	Sell	Date Time		Date Time		Outcome
Pair		Entry Price		Exit Price		Profit / Loss

Setup						

Mental State			Exit Condition			

Notes:						

Satoshis W/L			% of acct		USD Value	

Buy	Sell	Date Time		Date Time		Outcome
Pair		Entry Price		Exit Price		Profit / Loss

Setup						

Mental State			Exit Condition			

Notes:						

Satoshis W/L			% of acct		USD Value	

CRYPTO CURRENCY TRADING TRACKER

Buy	Sell	Date Time		Date Time		Outcome
Pair		Entry Price		Exit Price		Profit / Loss

Setup

Mental State	Exit Condition

Notes:

Satoshis W/L		% of acct		USD Value	

Buy	Sell	Date Time		Date Time		Outcome
Pair		Entry Price		Exit Price		Profit / Loss

Setup

Mental State	Exit Condition

Notes:

Satoshis W/L		% of acct		USD Value	

Buy	Sell	Date Time		Date Time		Outcome
Pair		Entry Price		Exit Price		Profit / Loss

Setup

Mental State	Exit Condition

Notes:

Satoshis W/L		% of acct		USD Value	

CRYPTO CURRENCY TRADING TRACKER

Buy	Sell	Date Time		Date Time		Outcome
Pair		Entry Price		Exit Price		Profit / Loss

Setup

Mental State	Exit Condition

Notes:

Satoshis W/L		% of acct		USD Value	

Buy	Sell	Date Time		Date Time		Outcome
Pair		Entry Price		Exit Price		Profit / Loss

Setup

Mental State	Exit Condition

Notes:

Satoshis W/L		% of acct		USD Value	

Buy	Sell	Date Time		Date Time		Outcome
Pair		Entry Price		Exit Price		Profit / Loss

Setup

Mental State	Exit Condition

Notes:

Satoshis W/L		% of acct		USD Value	

CRYPTO CURRENCY TRADING TRACKER

Buy	Sell	Date Time		Date Time		Outcome
Pair		Entry Price		Exit Price		Profit / Loss

Setup

Mental State		Exit Condition	

Notes:

Satoshis W/L		% of acct		USD Value	

Buy	Sell	Date Time		Date Time		Outcome
Pair		Entry Price		Exit Price		Profit / Loss

Setup

Mental State		Exit Condition	

Notes:

Satoshis W/L		% of acct		USD Value	

Buy	Sell	Date Time		Date Time		Outcome
Pair		Entry Price		Exit Price		Profit / Loss

Setup

Mental State		Exit Condition	

Notes:

Satoshis W/L		% of acct		USD Value	

CRYPTO CURRENCY TRADING TRACKER

Buy	Sell	Date Time		Date Time		Outcome
Pair		Entry Price		Exit Price		Profit / Loss
Setup						
Mental State			Exit Condition			
Notes:						
Satoshis W/L		% of acct		USD Value		

Buy	Sell	Date Time		Date Time		Outcome
Pair		Entry Price		Exit Price		Profit / Loss
Setup						
Mental State			Exit Condition			
Notes:						
Satoshis W/L		% of acct		USD Value		

Buy	Sell	Date Time		Date Time		Outcome
Pair		Entry Price		Exit Price		Profit / Loss
Setup						
Mental State			Exit Condition			
Notes:						
Satoshis W/L		% of acct		USD Value		

CRYPTO CURRENCY TRADING TRACKER

Buy	Sell	Date Time		Date Time		Outcome
Pair		Entry Price		Exit Price		Profit / Loss

Setup

Mental State		Exit Condition	

Notes:

Satoshis W/L		% of acct		USD Value	

Buy	Sell	Date Time		Date Time		Outcome
Pair		Entry Price		Exit Price		Profit / Loss

Setup

Mental State		Exit Condition	

Notes:

Satoshis W/L		% of acct		USD Value	

Buy	Sell	Date Time		Date Time		Outcome
Pair		Entry Price		Exit Price		Profit / Loss

Setup

Mental State		Exit Condition	

Notes:

Satoshis W/L		% of acct		USD Value	

CRYPTO CURRENCY TRADING TRACKER

Buy	Sell	Date Time		Date Time		Outcome
Pair		Entry Price		Exit Price		Profit / Loss

Setup

Mental State	Exit Condition

Notes:

Satoshis W/L		% of acct		USD Value	

Buy	Sell	Date Time		Date Time		Outcome
Pair		Entry Price		Exit Price		Profit / Loss

Setup

Mental State	Exit Condition

Notes:

Satoshis W/L		% of acct		USD Value	

Buy	Sell	Date Time		Date Time		Outcome
Pair		Entry Price		Exit Price		Profit / Loss

Setup

Mental State	Exit Condition

Notes:

Satoshis W/L		% of acct		USD Value	

CRYPTO CURRENCY TRADING TRACKER

Buy	Sell	Date Time		Date Time		Outcome
Pair		Entry Price		Exit Price		Profit / Loss

Setup

Mental State		Exit Condition	

Notes:

Satoshis W/L		% of acct		USD Value	

Buy	Sell	Date Time		Date Time		Outcome
Pair		Entry Price		Exit Price		Profit / Loss

Setup

Mental State		Exit Condition	

Notes:

Satoshis W/L		% of acct		USD Value	

Buy	Sell	Date Time		Date Time		Outcome
Pair		Entry Price		Exit Price		Profit / Loss

Setup

Mental State		Exit Condition	

Notes:

Satoshis W/L		% of acct		USD Value	

CRYPTO CURRENCY TRADING TRACKER

Buy	Sell	Date Time		Date Time		Outcome
Pair		Entry Price		Exit Price		Profit / Loss
Setup						
Mental State			Exit Condition			
Notes:						
Satoshis W/L		% of acct		USD Value		

Buy	Sell	Date Time		Date Time		Outcome
Pair		Entry Price		Exit Price		Profit / Loss
Setup						
Mental State			Exit Condition			
Notes:						
Satoshis W/L		% of acct		USD Value		

Buy	Sell	Date Time		Date Time		Outcome
Pair		Entry Price		Exit Price		Profit / Loss
Setup						
Mental State			Exit Condition			
Notes:						
Satoshis W/L		% of acct		USD Value		

CRYPTO CURRENCY TRADING TRACKER

Buy	Sell	Date Time		Date Time		Outcome
Pair		Entry Price		Exit Price		Profit / Loss

Setup

| Mental State | | Exit Condition | |

Notes:

| Satoshis W/L | | % of acct | | USD Value | |

Buy	Sell	Date Time		Date Time		Outcome
Pair		Entry Price		Exit Price		Profit / Loss

Setup

| Mental State | | Exit Condition | |

Notes:

| Satoshis W/L | | % of acct | | USD Value | |

Buy	Sell	Date Time		Date Time		Outcome
Pair		Entry Price		Exit Price		Profit / Loss

Setup

| Mental State | | Exit Condition | |

Notes:

| Satoshis W/L | | % of acct | | USD Value | |

CRYPTO CURRENCY TRADING TRACKER

Buy	Sell	Date Time		Date Time		Outcome
Pair		Entry Price		Exit Price		Profit / Loss
Setup						
Mental State			Exit Condition			
Notes:						
Satoshis W/L		% of acct		USD Value		

Buy	Sell	Date Time		Date Time		Outcome
Pair		Entry Price		Exit Price		Profit / Loss
Setup						
Mental State			Exit Condition			
Notes:						
Satoshis W/L		% of acct		USD Value		

Buy	Sell	Date Time		Date Time		Outcome
Pair		Entry Price		Exit Price		Profit / Loss
Setup						
Mental State			Exit Condition			
Notes:						
Satoshis W/L		% of acct		USD Value		

CRYPTO CURRENCY TRADING TRACKER

Buy	Sell	Date Time		Date Time		Outcome
Pair		Entry Price		Exit Price		Profit / Loss

Setup

Mental State	Exit Condition

Notes:

Satoshis W/L		% of acct		USD Value	

Buy	Sell	Date Time		Date Time		Outcome
Pair		Entry Price		Exit Price		Profit / Loss

Setup

Mental State	Exit Condition

Notes:

Satoshis W/L		% of acct		USD Value	

Buy	Sell	Date Time		Date Time		Outcome
Pair		Entry Price		Exit Price		Profit / Loss

Setup

Mental State	Exit Condition

Notes:

Satoshis W/L		% of acct		USD Value	

CRYPTO CURRENCY TRADING TRACKER

Buy	Sell	Date Time		Date Time		Outcome
Pair		Entry Price		Exit Price		Profit / Loss

Setup

Mental State	Exit Condition

Notes:

Satoshis W/L		% of acct		USD Value	

Buy	Sell	Date Time		Date Time		Outcome
Pair		Entry Price		Exit Price		Profit / Loss

Setup

Mental State	Exit Condition

Notes:

Satoshis W/L		% of acct		USD Value	

Buy	Sell	Date Time		Date Time		Outcome
Pair		Entry Price		Exit Price		Profit / Loss

Setup

Mental State	Exit Condition

Notes:

Satoshis W/L		% of acct		USD Value	

CRYPTO CURRENCY TRADING TRACKER

Buy	Sell	Date Time		Date Time		Outcome
Pair		Entry Price		Exit Price		Profit / Loss
Setup						
Mental State			Exit Condition			
Notes:						
Satoshis W/L			% of acct		USD Value	

Buy	Sell	Date Time		Date Time		Outcome
Pair		Entry Price		Exit Price		Profit / Loss
Setup						
Mental State			Exit Condition			
Notes:						
Satoshis W/L			% of acct		USD Value	

Buy	Sell	Date Time		Date Time		Outcome
Pair		Entry Price		Exit Price		Profit / Loss
Setup						
Mental State			Exit Condition			
Notes:						
Satoshis W/L			% of acct		USD Value	

CRYPTO CURRENCY TRADING TRACKER

Buy	Sell	Date Time		Date Time		Outcome
Pair		Entry Price		Exit Price		Profit / Loss
Setup						
Mental State			Exit Condition			
Notes:						
Satoshis W/L		% of acct		USD Value		

Buy	Sell	Date Time		Date Time		Outcome
Pair		Entry Price		Exit Price		Profit / Loss
Setup						
Mental State			Exit Condition			
Notes:						
Satoshis W/L		% of acct		USD Value		

Buy	Sell	Date Time		Date Time		Outcome
Pair		Entry Price		Exit Price		Profit / Loss
Setup						
Mental State			Exit Condition			
Notes:						
Satoshis W/L		% of acct		USD Value		

CRYPTO CURRENCY TRADING TRACKER

Buy	Sell	Date Time		Date Time		Outcome
Pair		Entry Price		Exit Price		Profit / Loss

Setup

Mental State	Exit Condition

Notes:

Satoshis W/L		% of acct		USD Value	

Buy	Sell	Date Time		Date Time		Outcome
Pair		Entry Price		Exit Price		Profit / Loss

Setup

Mental State	Exit Condition

Notes:

Satoshis W/L		% of acct		USD Value	

Buy	Sell	Date Time		Date Time		Outcome
Pair		Entry Price		Exit Price		Profit / Loss

Setup

Mental State	Exit Condition

Notes:

Satoshis W/L		% of acct		USD Value	

CRYPTO CURRENCY TRADING TRACKER

Buy	Sell	Date Time		Date Time		Outcome
Pair		Entry Price		Exit Price		Profit / Loss
Setup						
Mental State			Exit Condition			
Notes:						
Satoshis W/L			% of acct		USD Value	

Buy	Sell	Date Time		Date Time		Outcome
Pair		Entry Price		Exit Price		Profit / Loss
Setup						
Mental State			Exit Condition			
Notes:						
Satoshis W/L			% of acct		USD Value	

Buy	Sell	Date Time		Date Time		Outcome
Pair		Entry Price		Exit Price		Profit / Loss
Setup						
Mental State			Exit Condition			
Notes:						
Satoshis W/L			% of acct		USD Value	

CRYPTO CURRENCY TRADING TRACKER

Buy	Sell	Date Time		Date Time		Outcome
Pair		Entry Price		Exit Price		Profit / Loss

Setup

Mental State		Exit Condition	

Notes:

Satoshis W/L		% of acct		USD Value	

Buy	Sell	Date Time		Date Time		Outcome
Pair		Entry Price		Exit Price		Profit / Loss

Setup

Mental State		Exit Condition	

Notes:

Satoshis W/L		% of acct		USD Value	

Buy	Sell	Date Time		Date Time		Outcome
Pair		Entry Price		Exit Price		Profit / Loss

Setup

Mental State		Exit Condition	

Notes:

Satoshis W/L		% of acct		USD Value	

CRYPTO CURRENCY TRADING TRACKER

Buy	Sell	Date Time		Date Time		Outcome
Pair		Entry Price		Exit Price		Profit / Loss

Setup

Mental State		Exit Condition	

Notes:

Satoshis W/L		% of acct		USD Value	

Buy	Sell	Date Time		Date Time		Outcome
Pair		Entry Price		Exit Price		Profit / Loss

Setup

Mental State		Exit Condition	

Notes:

Satoshis W/L		% of acct		USD Value	

Buy	Sell	Date Time		Date Time		Outcome
Pair		Entry Price		Exit Price		Profit / Loss

Setup

Mental State		Exit Condition	

Notes:

Satoshis W/L		% of acct		USD Value	

CRYPTO CURRENCY TRADING TRACKER

Buy	Sell	Date Time		Date Time		Outcome
Pair		Entry Price		Exit Price		Profit / Loss

Setup

Mental State	Exit Condition

Notes:

Satoshis W/L		% of acct		USD Value	

Buy	Sell	Date Time		Date Time		Outcome
Pair		Entry Price		Exit Price		Profit / Loss

Setup

Mental State	Exit Condition

Notes:

Satoshis W/L		% of acct		USD Value	

Buy	Sell	Date Time		Date Time		Outcome
Pair		Entry Price		Exit Price		Profit / Loss

Setup

Mental State	Exit Condition

Notes:

Satoshis W/L		% of acct		USD Value	

CRYPTO CURRENCY TRADING TRACKER

Buy	Sell	Date Time		Date Time		Outcome
Pair		Entry Price		Exit Price		Profit / Loss
Setup						
Mental State			Exit Condition			
Notes:						
Satoshis W/L		% of acct		USD Value		

Buy	Sell	Date Time		Date Time		Outcome
Pair		Entry Price		Exit Price		Profit / Loss
Setup						
Mental State			Exit Condition			
Notes:						
Satoshis W/L		% of acct		USD Value		

Buy	Sell	Date Time		Date Time		Outcome
Pair		Entry Price		Exit Price		Profit / Loss
Setup						
Mental State			Exit Condition			
Notes:						
Satoshis W/L		% of acct		USD Value		

CRYPTO CURRENCY TRADING TRACKER

Buy	Sell	Date Time		Date Time		Outcome
Pair		Entry Price		Exit Price		Profit / Loss

Setup

Mental State	Exit Condition

Notes:

Satoshis W/L		% of acct		USD Value	

Buy	Sell	Date Time		Date Time		Outcome
Pair		Entry Price		Exit Price		Profit / Loss

Setup

Mental State	Exit Condition

Notes:

Satoshis W/L		% of acct		USD Value	

Buy	Sell	Date Time		Date Time		Outcome
Pair		Entry Price		Exit Price		Profit / Loss

Setup

Mental State	Exit Condition

Notes:

Satoshis W/L		% of acct		USD Value	

CRYPTO CURRENCY TRADING TRACKER

Buy	Sell	Date Time		Date Time		Outcome
Pair		Entry Price		Exit Price		Profit / Loss

Setup

Mental State	Exit Condition

Notes:

Satoshis W/L		% of acct		USD Value	

Buy	Sell	Date Time		Date Time		Outcome
Pair		Entry Price		Exit Price		Profit / Loss

Setup

Mental State	Exit Condition

Notes:

Satoshis W/L		% of acct		USD Value	

Buy	Sell	Date Time		Date Time		Outcome
Pair		Entry Price		Exit Price		Profit / Loss

Setup

Mental State	Exit Condition

Notes:

Satoshis W/L		% of acct		USD Value	

CRYPTO CURRENCY TRADING TRACKER

Buy	Sell	Date Time		Date Time		Outcome
Pair		Entry Price		Exit Price		Profit / Loss

Setup		

Mental State	Exit Condition

Notes:		

Satoshis W/L		% of acct		USD Value	

Buy	Sell	Date Time		Date Time		Outcome
Pair		Entry Price		Exit Price		Profit / Loss

Setup		

Mental State	Exit Condition

Notes:		

Satoshis W/L		% of acct		USD Value	

Buy	Sell	Date Time		Date Time		Outcome
Pair		Entry Price		Exit Price		Profit / Loss

Setup		

Mental State	Exit Condition

Notes:		

Satoshis W/L		% of acct		USD Value	

CRYPTO CURRENCY TRADING TRACKER

Buy	Sell	Date Time		Date Time		Outcome
Pair		Entry Price		Exit Price		Profit / Loss
Setup						
Mental State			Exit Condition			
Notes:						
Satoshis W/L		% of acct		USD Value		

Buy	Sell	Date Time		Date Time		Outcome
Pair		Entry Price		Exit Price		Profit / Loss
Setup						
Mental State			Exit Condition			
Notes:						
Satoshis W/L		% of acct		USD Value		

Buy	Sell	Date Time		Date Time		Outcome
Pair		Entry Price		Exit Price		Profit / Loss
Setup						
Mental State			Exit Condition			
Notes:						
Satoshis W/L		% of acct		USD Value		

CRYPTO CURRENCY TRADING TRACKER

Buy	Sell	Date Time		Date Time		Outcome
Pair		Entry Price		Exit Price		Profit / Loss
Setup						
Mental State			Exit Condition			
Notes:						
Satoshis W/L			% of acct		USD Value	

Buy	Sell	Date Time		Date Time		Outcome
Pair		Entry Price		Exit Price		Profit / Loss
Setup						
Mental State			Exit Condition			
Notes:						
Satoshis W/L			% of acct		USD Value	

Buy	Sell	Date Time		Date Time		Outcome
Pair		Entry Price		Exit Price		Profit / Loss
Setup						
Mental State			Exit Condition			
Notes:						
Satoshis W/L			% of acct		USD Value	

CRYPTO CURRENCY TRADING TRACKER

Buy	Sell	Date Time		Date Time		Outcome
Pair		Entry Price		Exit Price		Profit / Loss

Setup

Mental State	Exit Condition

Notes:

Satoshis W/L		% of acct		USD Value	

Buy	Sell	Date Time		Date Time		Outcome
Pair		Entry Price		Exit Price		Profit / Loss

Setup

Mental State	Exit Condition

Notes:

Satoshis W/L		% of acct		USD Value	

Buy	Sell	Date Time		Date Time		Outcome
Pair		Entry Price		Exit Price		Profit / Loss

Setup

Mental State	Exit Condition

Notes:

Satoshis W/L		% of acct		USD Value	

CRYPTO CURRENCY TRADING TRACKER

Buy	Sell	Date Time		Date Time		Outcome
Pair		Entry Price		Exit Price		Profit / Loss

Setup

Mental State	Exit Condition

Notes:

Satoshis W/L		% of acct		USD Value	

Buy	Sell	Date Time		Date Time		Outcome
Pair		Entry Price		Exit Price		Profit / Loss

Setup

Mental State	Exit Condition

Notes:

Satoshis W/L		% of acct		USD Value	

Buy	Sell	Date Time		Date Time		Outcome
Pair		Entry Price		Exit Price		Profit / Loss

Setup

Mental State	Exit Condition

Notes:

Satoshis W/L		% of acct		USD Value	

CRYPTO CURRENCY TRADING TRACKER

Buy	Sell	Date Time		Date Time		Outcome
Pair		Entry Price		Exit Price		Profit / Loss

Setup

Mental State	Exit Condition

Notes:

Satoshis W/L		% of acct		USD Value	

Buy	Sell	Date Time		Date Time		Outcome
Pair		Entry Price		Exit Price		Profit / Loss

Setup

Mental State	Exit Condition

Notes:

Satoshis W/L		% of acct		USD Value	

Buy	Sell	Date Time		Date Time		Outcome
Pair		Entry Price		Exit Price		Profit / Loss

Setup

Mental State	Exit Condition

Notes:

Satoshis W/L		% of acct		USD Value	

CRYPTO CURRENCY TRADING TRACKER

Buy	Sell	Date Time		Date Time		Outcome
Pair		Entry Price		Exit Price		Profit / Loss

Setup

Mental State	Exit Condition

Notes:

Satoshis W/L		% of acct		USD Value	

Buy	Sell	Date Time		Date Time		Outcome
Pair		Entry Price		Exit Price		Profit / Loss

Setup

Mental State	Exit Condition

Notes:

Satoshis W/L		% of acct		USD Value	

Buy	Sell	Date Time		Date Time		Outcome
Pair		Entry Price		Exit Price		Profit / Loss

Setup

Mental State	Exit Condition

Notes:

Satoshis W/L		% of acct		USD Value	

CRYPTO CURRENCY TRADING TRACKER

Buy	Sell	Date Time		Date Time		Outcome
Pair		Entry Price		Exit Price		Profit / Loss

Setup		

Mental State	Exit Condition

Notes:

Satoshis W/L		% of acct		USD Value	

Buy	Sell	Date Time		Date Time		Outcome
Pair		Entry Price		Exit Price		Profit / Loss

Setup		

Mental State	Exit Condition

Notes:

Satoshis W/L		% of acct		USD Value	

Buy	Sell	Date Time		Date Time		Outcome
Pair		Entry Price		Exit Price		Profit / Loss

Setup		

Mental State	Exit Condition

Notes:

Satoshis W/L		% of acct		USD Value	

CRYPTO CURRENCY TRADING TRACKER

Buy	Sell	Date Time		Date Time		Outcome
Pair		Entry Price		Exit Price		Profit / Loss
Setup						
Mental State			Exit Condition			
Notes:						
Satoshis W/L			% of acct		USD Value	

Buy	Sell	Date Time		Date Time		Outcome
Pair		Entry Price		Exit Price		Profit / Loss
Setup						
Mental State			Exit Condition			
Notes:						
Satoshis W/L			% of acct		USD Value	

Buy	Sell	Date Time		Date Time		Outcome
Pair		Entry Price		Exit Price		Profit / Loss
Setup						
Mental State			Exit Condition			
Notes:						
Satoshis W/L			% of acct		USD Value	

CRYPTO CURRENCY TRADING TRACKER

Buy	Sell	Date Time		Date Time		Outcome
Pair		Entry Price		Exit Price		Profit / Loss
Setup						
Mental State			Exit Condition			
Notes:						
Satoshis W/L			% of acct		USD Value	

Buy	Sell	Date Time		Date Time		Outcome
Pair		Entry Price		Exit Price		Profit / Loss
Setup						
Mental State			Exit Condition			
Notes:						
Satoshis W/L			% of acct		USD Value	

Buy	Sell	Date Time		Date Time		Outcome
Pair		Entry Price		Exit Price		Profit / Loss
Setup						
Mental State			Exit Condition			
Notes:						
Satoshis W/L			% of acct		USD Value	

CRYPTO CURRENCY TRADING TRACKER

Buy	Sell	Date Time		Date Time		Outcome
Pair		Entry Price		Exit Price		Profit / Loss

Setup

Mental State	Exit Condition

Notes:

Satoshis W/L		% of acct		USD Value	

Buy	Sell	Date Time		Date Time		Outcome
Pair		Entry Price		Exit Price		Profit / Loss

Setup

Mental State	Exit Condition

Notes:

Satoshis W/L		% of acct		USD Value	

Buy	Sell	Date Time		Date Time		Outcome
Pair		Entry Price		Exit Price		Profit / Loss

Setup

Mental State	Exit Condition

Notes:

Satoshis W/L		% of acct		USD Value	

CRYPTO CURRENCY TRADING TRACKER

Buy	Sell	Date Time		Date Time		Outcome
Pair		Entry Price		Exit Price		Profit / Loss

Setup						

Mental State			Exit Condition			

Notes:						

Satoshis W/L		% of acct		USD Value	

Buy	Sell	Date Time		Date Time		Outcome
Pair		Entry Price		Exit Price		Profit / Loss

Setup						

Mental State			Exit Condition			

Notes:						

Satoshis W/L		% of acct		USD Value	

Buy	Sell	Date Time		Date Time		Outcome
Pair		Entry Price		Exit Price		Profit / Loss

Setup						

Mental State			Exit Condition			

Notes:						

Satoshis W/L		% of acct		USD Value	

CRYPTO CURRENCY TRADING TRACKER

Buy	Sell	Date Time		Date Time		Outcome
Pair		Entry Price		Exit Price		Profit / Loss

Setup						
Mental State			Exit Condition			
Notes:						
Satoshis W/L		% of acct			USD Value	

Buy	Sell	Date Time		Date Time		Outcome
Pair		Entry Price		Exit Price		Profit / Loss

Setup						
Mental State			Exit Condition			
Notes:						
Satoshis W/L		% of acct			USD Value	

Buy	Sell	Date Time		Date Time		Outcome
Pair		Entry Price		Exit Price		Profit / Loss

Setup						
Mental State			Exit Condition			
Notes:						
Satoshis W/L		% of acct			USD Value	

CRYPTO CURRENCY TRADING TRACKER

Buy	Sell	Date Time		Date Time		Outcome
Pair		Entry Price		Exit Price		Profit / Loss

Setup			

Mental State		Exit Condition	

Notes:			

Satoshis W/L		% of acct		USD Value	

Buy	Sell	Date Time		Date Time		Outcome
Pair		Entry Price		Exit Price		Profit / Loss

Setup			

Mental State		Exit Condition	

Notes:			

Satoshis W/L		% of acct		USD Value	

Buy	Sell	Date Time		Date Time		Outcome
Pair		Entry Price		Exit Price		Profit / Loss

Setup			

Mental State		Exit Condition	

Notes:			

Satoshis W/L		% of acct		USD Value	

CRYPTO CURRENCY TRADING TRACKER

Buy	Sell	Date Time		Date Time		Outcome
Pair		Entry Price		Exit Price		Profit / Loss

Setup

Mental State	Exit Condition

Notes:

Satoshis W/L		% of acct		USD Value	

Buy	Sell	Date Time		Date Time		Outcome
Pair		Entry Price		Exit Price		Profit / Loss

Setup

Mental State	Exit Condition

Notes:

Satoshis W/L		% of acct		USD Value	

Buy	Sell	Date Time		Date Time		Outcome
Pair		Entry Price		Exit Price		Profit / Loss

Setup

Mental State	Exit Condition

Notes:

Satoshis W/L		% of acct		USD Value	

CRYPTO CURRENCY TRADING TRACKER

Buy	Sell	Date Time		Date Time		Outcome
Pair		Entry Price		Exit Price		Profit / Loss
Setup						
Mental State			Exit Condition			
Notes:						
Satoshis W/L			% of acct		USD Value	

Buy	Sell	Date Time		Date Time		Outcome
Pair		Entry Price		Exit Price		Profit / Loss
Setup						
Mental State			Exit Condition			
Notes:						
Satoshis W/L			% of acct		USD Value	

Buy	Sell	Date Time		Date Time		Outcome
Pair		Entry Price		Exit Price		Profit / Loss
Setup						
Mental State			Exit Condition			
Notes:						
Satoshis W/L			% of acct		USD Value	

CRYPTO CURRENCY TRADING TRACKER

Buy	Sell	Date Time		Date Time		Outcome	
Pair		Entry Price		Exit Price		Profit / Loss	
Setup							
Mental State			Exit Condition				
Notes:							
Satoshis W/L			% of acct			USD Value	

Buy	Sell	Date Time		Date Time		Outcome	
Pair		Entry Price		Exit Price		Profit / Loss	
Setup							
Mental State			Exit Condition				
Notes:							
Satoshis W/L			% of acct			USD Value	

Buy	Sell	Date Time		Date Time		Outcome	
Pair		Entry Price		Exit Price		Profit / Loss	
Setup							
Mental State			Exit Condition				
Notes:							
Satoshis W/L			% of acct			USD Value	

CRYPTO CURRENCY TRADING TRACKER

Buy	Sell	Date Time		Date Time		Outcome
Pair		Entry Price		Exit Price		Profit / Loss

Setup

Mental State	Exit Condition

Notes:

Satoshis W/L		% of acct		USD Value	

Buy	Sell	Date Time		Date Time		Outcome
Pair		Entry Price		Exit Price		Profit / Loss

Setup

Mental State	Exit Condition

Notes:

Satoshis W/L		% of acct		USD Value	

Buy	Sell	Date Time		Date Time		Outcome
Pair		Entry Price		Exit Price		Profit / Loss

Setup

Mental State	Exit Condition

Notes:

Satoshis W/L		% of acct		USD Value	

CRYPTO CURRENCY TRADING TRACKER

Buy	Sell	Date Time		Date Time		Outcome
Pair		Entry Price		Exit Price		Profit / Loss

Setup

Mental State	Exit Condition

Notes:

Satoshis W/L		% of acct		USD Value	

Buy	Sell	Date Time		Date Time		Outcome
Pair		Entry Price		Exit Price		Profit / Loss

Setup

Mental State	Exit Condition

Notes:

Satoshis W/L		% of acct		USD Value	

Buy	Sell	Date Time		Date Time		Outcome
Pair		Entry Price		Exit Price		Profit / Loss

Setup

Mental State	Exit Condition

Notes:

Satoshis W/L		% of acct		USD Value	

CRYPTO CURRENCY TRADING TRACKER

Buy	Sell	Date Time		Date Time		Outcome
Pair		Entry Price		Exit Price		Profit / Loss
Setup						
Mental State			Exit Condition			
Notes:						
Satoshis W/L		% of acct		USD Value		

Buy	Sell	Date Time		Date Time		Outcome
Pair		Entry Price		Exit Price		Profit / Loss
Setup						
Mental State			Exit Condition			
Notes:						
Satoshis W/L		% of acct		USD Value		

Buy	Sell	Date Time		Date Time		Outcome
Pair		Entry Price		Exit Price		Profit / Loss
Setup						
Mental State			Exit Condition			
Notes:						
Satoshis W/L		% of acct		USD Value		

CRYPTO CURRENCY TRADING TRACKER

Buy	Sell	Date Time		Date Time		Outcome	
Pair		Entry Price		Exit Price		Profit / Loss	

Setup

Mental State	Exit Condition

Notes:

Satoshis W/L		% of acct		USD Value	

Buy	Sell	Date Time		Date Time		Outcome	
Pair		Entry Price		Exit Price		Profit / Loss	

Setup

Mental State	Exit Condition

Notes:

Satoshis W/L		% of acct		USD Value	

Buy	Sell	Date Time		Date Time		Outcome	
Pair		Entry Price		Exit Price		Profit / Loss	

Setup

Mental State	Exit Condition

Notes:

Satoshis W/L		% of acct		USD Value	

CRYPTO CURRENCY TRADING TRACKER

Buy	Sell	Date Time		Date Time		Outcome
Pair		Entry Price		Exit Price		Profit / Loss

Setup

Mental State	Exit Condition

Notes:

Satoshis W/L		% of acct		USD Value	

Buy	Sell	Date Time		Date Time		Outcome
Pair		Entry Price		Exit Price		Profit / Loss

Setup

Mental State	Exit Condition

Notes:

Satoshis W/L		% of acct		USD Value	

Buy	Sell	Date Time		Date Time		Outcome
Pair		Entry Price		Exit Price		Profit / Loss

Setup

Mental State	Exit Condition

Notes:

Satoshis W/L		% of acct		USD Value	

CRYPTO CURRENCY TRADING TRACKER

Buy	Sell	Date Time		Date Time		Outcome
Pair		Entry Price		Exit Price		Profit / Loss

Setup						

Mental State			Exit Condition			

Notes:						

Satoshis W/L			% of acct		USD Value	

Buy	Sell	Date Time		Date Time		Outcome
Pair		Entry Price		Exit Price		Profit / Loss

Setup						

Mental State			Exit Condition			

Notes:						

Satoshis W/L			% of acct		USD Value	

Buy	Sell	Date Time		Date Time		Outcome
Pair		Entry Price		Exit Price		Profit / Loss

Setup						

Mental State			Exit Condition			

Notes:						

Satoshis W/L			% of acct		USD Value	

CRYPTO CURRENCY TRADING TRACKER

Buy	Sell	Date Time		Date Time		Outcome
Pair		Entry Price		Exit Price		Profit / Loss

Setup						
Mental State			Exit Condition			
Notes:						
Satoshis W/L		% of acct		USD Value		

Buy	Sell	Date Time		Date Time		Outcome
Pair		Entry Price		Exit Price		Profit / Loss

Setup						
Mental State			Exit Condition			
Notes:						
Satoshis W/L		% of acct		USD Value		

Buy	Sell	Date Time		Date Time		Outcome
Pair		Entry Price		Exit Price		Profit / Loss

Setup						
Mental State			Exit Condition			
Notes:						
Satoshis W/L		% of acct		USD Value		

CRYPTO CURRENCY TRADING TRACKER

Buy	Sell	Date Time		Date Time		Outcome
Pair		Entry Price		Exit Price		Profit / Loss

Setup

Mental State	Exit Condition

Notes:

Satoshis W/L		% of acct		USD Value	

Buy	Sell	Date Time		Date Time		Outcome
Pair		Entry Price		Exit Price		Profit / Loss

Setup

Mental State	Exit Condition

Notes:

Satoshis W/L		% of acct		USD Value	

Buy	Sell	Date Time		Date Time		Outcome
Pair		Entry Price		Exit Price		Profit / Loss

Setup

Mental State	Exit Condition

Notes:

Satoshis W/L		% of acct		USD Value	

CRYPTO CURRENCY TRADING TRACKER

Buy	Sell	Date Time		Date Time		Outcome
Pair		Entry Price		Exit Price		Profit / Loss

Setup

Mental State	Exit Condition

Notes:

Satoshis W/L		% of acct		USD Value	

Buy	Sell	Date Time		Date Time		Outcome
Pair		Entry Price		Exit Price		Profit / Loss

Setup

Mental State	Exit Condition

Notes:

Satoshis W/L		% of acct		USD Value	

Buy	Sell	Date Time		Date Time		Outcome
Pair		Entry Price		Exit Price		Profit / Loss

Setup

Mental State	Exit Condition

Notes:

Satoshis W/L		% of acct		USD Value	

CRYPTO CURRENCY TRADING TRACKER

Buy	Sell	Date Time		Date Time		Outcome
Pair		Entry Price		Exit Price		Profit / Loss

Setup

Mental State	Exit Condition

Notes:

Satoshis W/L		% of acct		USD Value	

Buy	Sell	Date Time		Date Time		Outcome
Pair		Entry Price		Exit Price		Profit / Loss

Setup

Mental State	Exit Condition

Notes:

Satoshis W/L		% of acct		USD Value	

Buy	Sell	Date Time		Date Time		Outcome
Pair		Entry Price		Exit Price		Profit / Loss

Setup

Mental State	Exit Condition

Notes:

Satoshis W/L		% of acct		USD Value	

CRYPTO CURRENCY TRADING TRACKER

Buy	Sell	Date Time		Date Time		Outcome
Pair		Entry Price		Exit Price		Profit / Loss

Setup

Mental State		Exit Condition	

Notes:

Satoshis W/L		% of acct		USD Value	

Buy	Sell	Date Time		Date Time		Outcome
Pair		Entry Price		Exit Price		Profit / Loss

Setup

Mental State		Exit Condition	

Notes:

Satoshis W/L		% of acct		USD Value	

Buy	Sell	Date Time		Date Time		Outcome
Pair		Entry Price		Exit Price		Profit / Loss

Setup

Mental State		Exit Condition	

Notes:

Satoshis W/L		% of acct		USD Value	

CRYPTO CURRENCY TRADING TRACKER

Buy	Sell	Date Time		Date Time		Outcome
Pair		Entry Price		Exit Price		Profit / Loss

Setup

Mental State		Exit Condition	

Notes:

Satoshis W/L		% of acct		USD Value	

Buy	Sell	Date Time		Date Time		Outcome
Pair		Entry Price		Exit Price		Profit / Loss

Setup

Mental State		Exit Condition	

Notes:

Satoshis W/L		% of acct		USD Value	

Buy	Sell	Date Time		Date Time		Outcome
Pair		Entry Price		Exit Price		Profit / Loss

Setup

Mental State		Exit Condition	

Notes:

Satoshis W/L		% of acct		USD Value	

CRYPTO CURRENCY TRADING TRACKER

Buy	Sell	Date Time		Date Time		Outcome
Pair		Entry Price		Exit Price		Profit / Loss

Setup

Mental State	Exit Condition

Notes:

Satoshis W/L		% of acct		USD Value	

Buy	Sell	Date Time		Date Time		Outcome
Pair		Entry Price		Exit Price		Profit / Loss

Setup

Mental State	Exit Condition

Notes:

Satoshis W/L		% of acct		USD Value	

Buy	Sell	Date Time		Date Time		Outcome
Pair		Entry Price		Exit Price		Profit / Loss

Setup

Mental State	Exit Condition

Notes:

Satoshis W/L		% of acct		USD Value	

CRYPTO CURRENCY TRADING TRACKER

Buy	Sell	Date Time		Date Time		Outcome
Pair		Entry Price		Exit Price		Profit / Loss

Setup

Mental State		Exit Condition	

Notes:

Satoshis W/L		% of acct		USD Value	

Buy	Sell	Date Time		Date Time		Outcome
Pair		Entry Price		Exit Price		Profit / Loss

Setup

Mental State		Exit Condition	

Notes:

Satoshis W/L		% of acct		USD Value	

Buy	Sell	Date Time		Date Time		Outcome
Pair		Entry Price		Exit Price		Profit / Loss

Setup

Mental State		Exit Condition	

Notes:

Satoshis W/L		% of acct		USD Value	

CRYPTO CURRENCY TRADING TRACKER

Buy	Sell	Date Time		Date Time		Outcome
Pair		Entry Price		Exit Price		Profit / Loss
Setup						
Mental State			Exit Condition			
Notes:						
Satoshis W/L		% of acct		USD Value		

Buy	Sell	Date Time		Date Time		Outcome
Pair		Entry Price		Exit Price		Profit / Loss
Setup						
Mental State			Exit Condition			
Notes:						
Satoshis W/L		% of acct		USD Value		

Buy	Sell	Date Time		Date Time		Outcome
Pair		Entry Price		Exit Price		Profit / Loss
Setup						
Mental State			Exit Condition			
Notes:						
Satoshis W/L		% of acct		USD Value		

CRYPTO CURRENCY TRADING TRACKER

Buy	Sell	Date Time		Date Time		Outcome	
Pair		Entry Price		Exit Price		Profit / Loss	
Setup							
Mental State			Exit Condition				
Notes:							
Satoshis W/L			% of acct			USD Value	

Buy	Sell	Date Time		Date Time		Outcome	
Pair		Entry Price		Exit Price		Profit / Loss	
Setup							
Mental State			Exit Condition				
Notes:							
Satoshis W/L			% of acct			USD Value	

Buy	Sell	Date Time		Date Time		Outcome	
Pair		Entry Price		Exit Price		Profit / Loss	
Setup							
Mental State			Exit Condition				
Notes:							
Satoshis W/L			% of acct			USD Value	

CRYPTO CURRENCY TRADING TRACKER

Buy	Sell	Date Time		Date Time		Outcome
Pair		Entry Price		Exit Price		Profit / Loss

Setup

Mental State	Exit Condition

Notes:

Satoshis W/L		% of acct		USD Value	

Buy	Sell	Date Time		Date Time		Outcome
Pair		Entry Price		Exit Price		Profit / Loss

Setup

Mental State	Exit Condition

Notes:

Satoshis W/L		% of acct		USD Value	

Buy	Sell	Date Time		Date Time		Outcome
Pair		Entry Price		Exit Price		Profit / Loss

Setup

Mental State	Exit Condition

Notes:

Satoshis W/L		% of acct		USD Value	

CRYPTO CURRENCY TRADING TRACKER

Buy	Sell	Date Time		Date Time		Outcome
Pair		Entry Price		Exit Price		Profit / Loss
Setup						
Mental State			Exit Condition			
Notes:						
Satoshis W/L			% of acct		USD Value	

Buy	Sell	Date Time		Date Time		Outcome
Pair		Entry Price		Exit Price		Profit / Loss
Setup						
Mental State			Exit Condition			
Notes:						
Satoshis W/L			% of acct		USD Value	

Buy	Sell	Date Time		Date Time		Outcome
Pair		Entry Price		Exit Price		Profit / Loss
Setup						
Mental State			Exit Condition			
Notes:						
Satoshis W/L			% of acct		USD Value	

CRYPTO CURRENCY TRADING TRACKER

Buy	Sell	Date Time		Date Time		Outcome
Pair		Entry Price		Exit Price		Profit / Loss

Setup

Mental State	Exit Condition

Notes:

Satoshis W/L		% of acct		USD Value	

Buy	Sell	Date Time		Date Time		Outcome
Pair		Entry Price		Exit Price		Profit / Loss

Setup

Mental State	Exit Condition

Notes:

Satoshis W/L		% of acct		USD Value	

Buy	Sell	Date Time		Date Time		Outcome
Pair		Entry Price		Exit Price		Profit / Loss

Setup

Mental State	Exit Condition

Notes:

Satoshis W/L		% of acct		USD Value	

CRYPTO CURRENCY TRADING TRACKER

Buy	Sell	Date Time		Date Time		Outcome
Pair		Entry Price		Exit Price		Profit / Loss

Setup						

Mental State			Exit Condition			

Notes:						

Satoshis W/L		% of acct		USD Value	

Buy	Sell	Date Time		Date Time		Outcome
Pair		Entry Price		Exit Price		Profit / Loss

Setup						

Mental State			Exit Condition			

Notes:						

Satoshis W/L		% of acct		USD Value	

Buy	Sell	Date Time		Date Time		Outcome
Pair		Entry Price		Exit Price		Profit / Loss

Setup						

Mental State			Exit Condition			

Notes:						

Satoshis W/L		% of acct		USD Value	

CRYPTO CURRENCY TRADING TRACKER

Buy	Sell	Date Time		Date Time		Outcome
Pair		Entry Price		Exit Price		Profit / Loss

Setup

Mental State	Exit Condition

Notes:

Satoshis W/L		% of acct		USD Value	

Buy	Sell	Date Time		Date Time		Outcome
Pair		Entry Price		Exit Price		Profit / Loss

Setup

Mental State	Exit Condition

Notes:

Satoshis W/L		% of acct		USD Value	

Buy	Sell	Date Time		Date Time		Outcome
Pair		Entry Price		Exit Price		Profit / Loss

Setup

Mental State	Exit Condition

Notes:

Satoshis W/L		% of acct		USD Value	

CRYPTO CURRENCY TRADING TRACKER

Buy	Sell	Date Time		Date Time		Outcome
Pair		Entry Price		Exit Price		Profit / Loss

Setup	

Mental State	Exit Condition

Notes:

Satoshis W/L		% of acct		USD Value	

Buy	Sell	Date Time		Date Time		Outcome
Pair		Entry Price		Exit Price		Profit / Loss

Setup	

Mental State	Exit Condition

Notes:

Satoshis W/L		% of acct		USD Value	

Buy	Sell	Date Time		Date Time		Outcome
Pair		Entry Price		Exit Price		Profit / Loss

Setup	

Mental State	Exit Condition

Notes:

Satoshis W/L		% of acct		USD Value	

CRYPTO CURRENCY TRADING TRACKER

Buy	Sell	Date Time		Date Time		Outcome
Pair		Entry Price		Exit Price		Profit / Loss

Setup	

Mental State	Exit Condition

Notes:

Satoshis W/L		% of acct		USD Value	

Buy	Sell	Date Time		Date Time		Outcome
Pair		Entry Price		Exit Price		Profit / Loss

Setup	

Mental State	Exit Condition

Notes:

Satoshis W/L		% of acct		USD Value	

Buy	Sell	Date Time		Date Time		Outcome
Pair		Entry Price		Exit Price		Profit / Loss

Setup	

Mental State	Exit Condition

Notes:

Satoshis W/L		% of acct		USD Value	

CRYPTO CURRENCY TRADING TRACKER

Buy	Sell	Date Time		Date Time		Outcome
Pair		Entry Price		Exit Price		Profit / Loss

Setup

Mental State		Exit Condition	

Notes:

Satoshis W/L		% of acct		USD Value	

Buy	Sell	Date Time		Date Time		Outcome
Pair		Entry Price		Exit Price		Profit / Loss

Setup

Mental State		Exit Condition	

Notes:

Satoshis W/L		% of acct		USD Value	

Buy	Sell	Date Time		Date Time		Outcome
Pair		Entry Price		Exit Price		Profit / Loss

Setup

Mental State		Exit Condition	

Notes:

Satoshis W/L		% of acct		USD Value	

CRYPTO CURRENCY TRADING TRACKER

Buy	Sell	Date Time		Date Time		Outcome
Pair		Entry Price		Exit Price		Profit / Loss

Setup

Mental State	Exit Condition

Notes:

Satoshis W/L		% of acct		USD Value	

Buy	Sell	Date Time		Date Time		Outcome
Pair		Entry Price		Exit Price		Profit / Loss

Setup

Mental State	Exit Condition

Notes:

Satoshis W/L		% of acct		USD Value	

Buy	Sell	Date Time		Date Time		Outcome
Pair		Entry Price		Exit Price		Profit / Loss

Setup

Mental State	Exit Condition

Notes:

Satoshis W/L		% of acct		USD Value	

CRYPTO CURRENCY TRADING TRACKER

Buy	Sell	Date Time		Date Time		Outcome
Pair		Entry Price		Exit Price		Profit / Loss

Setup

Mental State		Exit Condition	

Notes:

Satoshis W/L		% of acct		USD Value	

Buy	Sell	Date Time		Date Time		Outcome
Pair		Entry Price		Exit Price		Profit / Loss

Setup

Mental State		Exit Condition	

Notes:

Satoshis W/L		% of acct		USD Value	

Buy	Sell	Date Time		Date Time		Outcome
Pair		Entry Price		Exit Price		Profit / Loss

Setup

Mental State		Exit Condition	

Notes:

Satoshis W/L		% of acct		USD Value	

CRYPTO CURRENCY TRADING TRACKER

Buy	Sell	Date Time		Date Time		Outcome
Pair		Entry Price		Exit Price		Profit / Loss
Setup						
Mental State			Exit Condition			
Notes:						
Satoshis W/L			% of acct		USD Value	

Buy	Sell	Date Time		Date Time		Outcome
Pair		Entry Price		Exit Price		Profit / Loss
Setup						
Mental State			Exit Condition			
Notes:						
Satoshis W/L			% of acct		USD Value	

Buy	Sell	Date Time		Date Time		Outcome
Pair		Entry Price		Exit Price		Profit / Loss
Setup						
Mental State			Exit Condition			
Notes:						
Satoshis W/L			% of acct		USD Value	

CRYPTO CURRENCY TRADING TRACKER

Buy	Sell	Date Time		Date Time		Outcome
Pair		Entry Price		Exit Price		Profit / Loss

Setup						
Mental State			Exit Condition			
Notes:						
Satoshis W/L		% of acct		USD Value		

Buy	Sell	Date Time		Date Time		Outcome
Pair		Entry Price		Exit Price		Profit / Loss

Setup						
Mental State			Exit Condition			
Notes:						
Satoshis W/L		% of acct		USD Value		

Buy	Sell	Date Time		Date Time		Outcome
Pair		Entry Price		Exit Price		Profit / Loss

Setup						
Mental State			Exit Condition			
Notes:						
Satoshis W/L		% of acct		USD Value		

CRYPTO CURRENCY TRADING TRACKER

Buy	Sell	Date Time		Date Time		Outcome
Pair		Entry Price		Exit Price		Profit / Loss
Setup						
Mental State			Exit Condition			
Notes:						
Satoshis W/L		% of acct		USD Value		

Buy	Sell	Date Time		Date Time		Outcome
Pair		Entry Price		Exit Price		Profit / Loss
Setup						
Mental State			Exit Condition			
Notes:						
Satoshis W/L		% of acct		USD Value		

Buy	Sell	Date Time		Date Time		Outcome
Pair		Entry Price		Exit Price		Profit / Loss
Setup						
Mental State			Exit Condition			
Notes:						
Satoshis W/L		% of acct		USD Value		

CRYPTO CURRENCY TRADING TRACKER

Buy	Sell	Date Time		Date Time		Outcome
Pair		Entry Price		Exit Price		Profit / Loss

Setup

Mental State		Exit Condition	

Notes:

Satoshis W/L		% of acct		USD Value	

Buy	Sell	Date Time		Date Time		Outcome
Pair		Entry Price		Exit Price		Profit / Loss

Setup

Mental State		Exit Condition	

Notes:

Satoshis W/L		% of acct		USD Value	

Buy	Sell	Date Time		Date Time		Outcome
Pair		Entry Price		Exit Price		Profit / Loss

Setup

Mental State		Exit Condition	

Notes:

Satoshis W/L		% of acct		USD Value	

CRYPTO CURRENCY TRADING TRACKER

Buy	Sell	Date Time		Date Time		Outcome
Pair		Entry Price		Exit Price		Profit / Loss

Setup		

Mental State	Exit Condition

Notes:

Satoshis W/L		% of acct		USD Value	

Buy	Sell	Date Time		Date Time		Outcome
Pair		Entry Price		Exit Price		Profit / Loss

Setup		

Mental State	Exit Condition

Notes:

Satoshis W/L		% of acct		USD Value	

Buy	Sell	Date Time		Date Time		Outcome
Pair		Entry Price		Exit Price		Profit / Loss

Setup		

Mental State	Exit Condition

Notes:

Satoshis W/L		% of acct		USD Value	

CRYPTO CURRENCY TRADING TRACKER

Buy	Sell	Date Time		Date Time		Outcome
Pair		Entry Price		Exit Price		Profit / Loss

Setup

Mental State	Exit Condition

Notes:

Satoshis W/L		% of acct		USD Value	

Buy	Sell	Date Time		Date Time		Outcome
Pair		Entry Price		Exit Price		Profit / Loss

Setup

Mental State	Exit Condition

Notes:

Satoshis W/L		% of acct		USD Value	

Buy	Sell	Date Time		Date Time		Outcome
Pair		Entry Price		Exit Price		Profit / Loss

Setup

Mental State	Exit Condition

Notes:

Satoshis W/L		% of acct		USD Value	

CRYPTO CURRENCY TRADING TRACKER

Buy	Sell	Date Time		Date Time		Outcome
Pair		Entry Price		Exit Price		Profit / Loss
Setup						
Mental State			Exit Condition			
Notes:						
Satoshis W/L		% of acct		USD Value		

Buy	Sell	Date Time		Date Time		Outcome
Pair		Entry Price		Exit Price		Profit / Loss
Setup						
Mental State			Exit Condition			
Notes:						
Satoshis W/L		% of acct		USD Value		

Buy	Sell	Date Time		Date Time		Outcome
Pair		Entry Price		Exit Price		Profit / Loss
Setup						
Mental State			Exit Condition			
Notes:						
Satoshis W/L		% of acct		USD Value		

CRYPTO CURRENCY TRADING TRACKER

Buy	Sell	Date Time		Date Time		Outcome
Pair		Entry Price		Exit Price		Profit / Loss
Setup						
Mental State			Exit Condition			
Notes:						
Satoshis W/L			% of acct		USD Value	

Buy	Sell	Date Time		Date Time		Outcome
Pair		Entry Price		Exit Price		Profit / Loss
Setup						
Mental State			Exit Condition			
Notes:						
Satoshis W/L			% of acct		USD Value	

Buy	Sell	Date Time		Date Time		Outcome
Pair		Entry Price		Exit Price		Profit / Loss
Setup						
Mental State			Exit Condition			
Notes:						
Satoshis W/L			% of acct		USD Value	

CRYPTO CURRENCY TRADING TRACKER

Buy	Sell	Date Time		Date Time		Outcome
Pair		Entry Price		Exit Price		Profit / Loss

Setup

Mental State	Exit Condition

Notes:

Satoshis W/L		% of acct		USD Value	

Buy	Sell	Date Time		Date Time		Outcome
Pair		Entry Price		Exit Price		Profit / Loss

Setup

Mental State	Exit Condition

Notes:

Satoshis W/L		% of acct		USD Value	

Buy	Sell	Date Time		Date Time		Outcome
Pair		Entry Price		Exit Price		Profit / Loss

Setup

Mental State	Exit Condition

Notes:

Satoshis W/L		% of acct		USD Value	

CRYPTO CURRENCY TRADING TRACKER

Buy	Sell	Date Time		Date Time		Outcome
Pair		Entry Price		Exit Price		Profit / Loss
Setup						
Mental State			Exit Condition			
Notes:						
Satoshis W/L			% of acct		USD Value	

Buy	Sell	Date Time		Date Time		Outcome
Pair		Entry Price		Exit Price		Profit / Loss
Setup						
Mental State			Exit Condition			
Notes:						
Satoshis W/L			% of acct		USD Value	

Buy	Sell	Date Time		Date Time		Outcome
Pair		Entry Price		Exit Price		Profit / Loss
Setup						
Mental State			Exit Condition			
Notes:						
Satoshis W/L			% of acct		USD Value	

CRYPTO CURRENCY TRADING TRACKER

Buy	Sell	Date Time		Date Time		Outcome
Pair		Entry Price		Exit Price		Profit / Loss

Setup		

Mental State		Exit Condition	

Notes:		

Satoshis W/L		% of acct		USD Value	

Buy	Sell	Date Time		Date Time		Outcome
Pair		Entry Price		Exit Price		Profit / Loss

Setup		

Mental State		Exit Condition	

Notes:		

Satoshis W/L		% of acct		USD Value	

Buy	Sell	Date Time		Date Time		Outcome
Pair		Entry Price		Exit Price		Profit / Loss

Setup		

Mental State		Exit Condition	

Notes:		

Satoshis W/L		% of acct		USD Value	

CRYPTO CURRENCY TRADING TRACKER

Buy	Sell	Date Time		Date Time		Outcome
Pair		Entry Price		Exit Price		Profit / Loss

Setup

Mental State	Exit Condition

Notes:

Satoshis W/L		% of acct		USD Value	

Buy	Sell	Date Time		Date Time		Outcome
Pair		Entry Price		Exit Price		Profit / Loss

Setup

Mental State	Exit Condition

Notes:

Satoshis W/L		% of acct		USD Value	

Buy	Sell	Date Time		Date Time		Outcome
Pair		Entry Price		Exit Price		Profit / Loss

Setup

Mental State	Exit Condition

Notes:

Satoshis W/L		% of acct		USD Value	

CRYPTO CURRENCY TRADING TRACKER

Buy	Sell	Date Time		Date Time		Outcome
Pair		Entry Price		Exit Price		Profit / Loss

Setup			

Mental State		Exit Condition	

Notes:

Satoshis W/L		% of acct		USD Value	

Buy	Sell	Date Time		Date Time		Outcome
Pair		Entry Price		Exit Price		Profit / Loss

Setup			

Mental State		Exit Condition	

Notes:

Satoshis W/L		% of acct		USD Value	

Buy	Sell	Date Time		Date Time		Outcome
Pair		Entry Price		Exit Price		Profit / Loss

Setup			

Mental State		Exit Condition	

Notes:

Satoshis W/L		% of acct		USD Value	

CRYPTO CURRENCY TRADING TRACKER

Buy	Sell	Date Time		Date Time		Outcome
Pair		Entry Price		Exit Price		Profit / Loss

Setup						

Mental State			Exit Condition			

Notes:						

Satoshis W/L			% of acct		USD Value	

Buy	Sell	Date Time		Date Time		Outcome
Pair		Entry Price		Exit Price		Profit / Loss

Setup						

Mental State			Exit Condition			

Notes:						

Satoshis W/L			% of acct		USD Value	

Buy	Sell	Date Time		Date Time		Outcome
Pair		Entry Price		Exit Price		Profit / Loss

Setup						

Mental State			Exit Condition			

Notes:						

Satoshis W/L			% of acct		USD Value	

CRYPTO CURRENCY TRADING TRACKER

Buy	Sell	Date Time		Date Time		Outcome
Pair		Entry Price		Exit Price		Profit / Loss

Setup

Mental State	Exit Condition

Notes:

Satoshis W/L		% of acct		USD Value	

Buy	Sell	Date Time		Date Time		Outcome
Pair		Entry Price		Exit Price		Profit / Loss

Setup

Mental State	Exit Condition

Notes:

Satoshis W/L		% of acct		USD Value	

Buy	Sell	Date Time		Date Time		Outcome
Pair		Entry Price		Exit Price		Profit / Loss

Setup

Mental State	Exit Condition

Notes:

Satoshis W/L		% of acct		USD Value	

CRYPTO CURRENCY TRADING TRACKER

Buy	Sell	Date Time		Date Time		Outcome
Pair		Entry Price		Exit Price		Profit / Loss

Setup

Mental State		Exit Condition	

Notes:

Satoshis W/L		% of acct		USD Value	

Buy	Sell	Date Time		Date Time		Outcome
Pair		Entry Price		Exit Price		Profit / Loss

Setup

Mental State		Exit Condition	

Notes:

Satoshis W/L		% of acct		USD Value	

Buy	Sell	Date Time		Date Time		Outcome
Pair		Entry Price		Exit Price		Profit / Loss

Setup

Mental State		Exit Condition	

Notes:

Satoshis W/L		% of acct		USD Value	

CRYPTO CURRENCY TRADING TRACKER

Buy	Sell	Date Time		Date Time		Outcome
Pair		Entry Price		Exit Price		Profit / Loss

Setup			

Mental State		Exit Condition	

Notes:			

Satoshis W/L		% of acct		USD Value	

Buy	Sell	Date Time		Date Time		Outcome
Pair		Entry Price		Exit Price		Profit / Loss

Setup			

Mental State		Exit Condition	

Notes:			

Satoshis W/L		% of acct		USD Value	

Buy	Sell	Date Time		Date Time		Outcome
Pair		Entry Price		Exit Price		Profit / Loss

Setup			

Mental State		Exit Condition	

Notes:			

Satoshis W/L		% of acct		USD Value	

CRYPTO CURRENCY TRADING TRACKER

Buy	Sell	Date Time		Date Time		Outcome
Pair		Entry Price		Exit Price		Profit / Loss

Setup

Mental State	Exit Condition

Notes:

Satoshis W/L		% of acct		USD Value	

Buy	Sell	Date Time		Date Time		Outcome
Pair		Entry Price		Exit Price		Profit / Loss

Setup

Mental State	Exit Condition

Notes:

Satoshis W/L		% of acct		USD Value	

Buy	Sell	Date Time		Date Time		Outcome
Pair		Entry Price		Exit Price		Profit / Loss

Setup

Mental State	Exit Condition

Notes:

Satoshis W/L		% of acct		USD Value	

CRYPTO CURRENCY TRADING TRACKER

Buy	Sell	Date Time		Date Time		Outcome
Pair		Entry Price		Exit Price		Profit / Loss

Setup

Mental State	Exit Condition

Notes:

Satoshis W/L		% of acct		USD Value	

Buy	Sell	Date Time		Date Time		Outcome
Pair		Entry Price		Exit Price		Profit / Loss

Setup

Mental State	Exit Condition

Notes:

Satoshis W/L		% of acct		USD Value	

Buy	Sell	Date Time		Date Time		Outcome
Pair		Entry Price		Exit Price		Profit / Loss

Setup

Mental State	Exit Condition

Notes:

Satoshis W/L		% of acct		USD Value	

CRYPTO CURRENCY TRADING TRACKER

Buy	Sell	Date Time		Date Time		Outcome
Pair		Entry Price		Exit Price		Profit / Loss

Setup						

Mental State			Exit Condition			

Notes:						

Satoshis W/L		% of acct		USD Value	

Buy	Sell	Date Time		Date Time		Outcome
Pair		Entry Price		Exit Price		Profit / Loss

Setup						

Mental State			Exit Condition			

Notes:						

Satoshis W/L		% of acct		USD Value	

Buy	Sell	Date Time		Date Time		Outcome
Pair		Entry Price		Exit Price		Profit / Loss

Setup						

Mental State			Exit Condition			

Notes:						

Satoshis W/L		% of acct		USD Value	

CRYPTO CURRENCY TRADING TRACKER

Buy	Sell	Date Time		Date Time		Outcome
Pair		Entry Price		Exit Price		Profit / Loss

Setup	
Mental State	Exit Condition
Notes:	

Satoshis W/L		% of acct		USD Value	

Buy	Sell	Date Time		Date Time		Outcome
Pair		Entry Price		Exit Price		Profit / Loss

Setup	
Mental State	Exit Condition
Notes:	

Satoshis W/L		% of acct		USD Value	

Buy	Sell	Date Time		Date Time		Outcome
Pair		Entry Price		Exit Price		Profit / Loss

Setup	
Mental State	Exit Condition
Notes:	

Satoshis W/L		% of acct		USD Value	

CRYPTO CURRENCY TRADING TRACKER

Buy	Sell	Date Time		Date Time		Outcome
Pair		Entry Price		Exit Price		Profit / Loss

Setup

Mental State	Exit Condition

Notes:

Satoshis W/L		% of acct		USD Value	

Buy	Sell	Date Time		Date Time		Outcome
Pair		Entry Price		Exit Price		Profit / Loss

Setup

Mental State	Exit Condition

Notes:

Satoshis W/L		% of acct		USD Value	

Buy	Sell	Date Time		Date Time		Outcome
Pair		Entry Price		Exit Price		Profit / Loss

Setup

Mental State	Exit Condition

Notes:

Satoshis W/L		% of acct		USD Value	

www.ingramcontent.com/pod-product-compliance
Lightning Source LLC
Chambersburg PA
CBHW070846070326
40690CB00009B/1723